Missionary Pumpkins

Miracle Stories from God's Pumpkin Patch

By Cheryl Eric

D1411621

TEACH Services, Inc.
PUBLISHING
www.TEACHServices.com • (800) 367-1844

Copyright © 2022 Cheryl Erickson
Copyright © 2022 TEACH Services, Inc.
ISBN-13: 978-1-4796-1492-9 (Paperback)
ISBN-13: 978-1-4796-1493-6 (ePub)
Library of Congress Control Number: 2022903740

Unless otherwise indicated, all scripture is taken from the King James Version (KJV). Public Domain.

Scripture labeled (NKJV) is taken from the New King James Version®. Copyright © 1982 by Thomas Nelson. Used by permission. All rights reserved.

Published by

TEACH Services, Inc.
PUBLISHING
www.TEACHServices.com • (800) 367-1844

Table of Contents

Dedication

I would like to dedicate this book and its proceeds to the non-profit, international mission organization, Maranatha. Through them and my "missionary pumpkins" we have been able to build churches for communities in need in India. I wish to thank Maranatha for all that they have done and for allowing me to work hand in hand with them as we continue this project.

If you would like to find out more about this amazing organization and their endeavors in volunteer placement, church and school building, housing projects, and evangelism programs, please visit their website at the following link: https://maranatha.org/.

Introduction

I t was the year 2000. Farming had not been good for a few years, and my husband said to me, "Why don't you take that little seven-acre patch up on the hill by the house and experiment with some specialty crops and see if we can make some money in that way?" I looked into several different options, including herbs, lavender, and alfalfa. One day I called the county extension agent in Fargo and asked for his advice. He said that there was a lady in the area who had planted a quarter-acre of pumpkins, and she was having good success. He gave me her number, and she was more than happy to help me get started. That was the beginning of a twenty-one-year pumpkin career and my partnership with God.

That first year, I planted one acre of pumpkins, which amounted to 400 hills with five seeds per hill. It took three long days, and every muscle in my body cried out for mercy, but I was excited to see what would happen. I have always been an avid gardener, and this was just a big garden, right? It was thrilling to watch the plants grow, develop, and produce beautiful pumpkins. I sold all 1,100 of them to the local grocery store in Jamestown, North Dakota.

Although the pumpkin crop was good and the profit per acre was much higher than traditional crops, we could see that it was labor-intense, and we could never raise enough pumpkins to make a living. My husband said that I could use it for a mission project, but I didn't know what to give it to that first year. I saved my money, and when a church leader visited our church that winter and explained how the people in India were becoming interested in Christianity and were being baptized by the thousands but fell away if they didn't have a church to worship in, I knew what I wanted to do! I would build churches for these new believers.

In the beginning, $3,500 would build a church, and one year I even built two churches. Sometimes I would have a little extra money, and I built two more churches in Kenya and one in Nicaragua. Altogether, a handful of seeds turned into twenty-five churches! The smaller ones I had completely funded, and the larger ones I had helped fund.

When I learned that I would have to quit raising pumpkins after the 2020 harvest, I had an idea of how to keep earning money to build more churches—I would write a book and share what it was like to be part-ners with God. I couldn't control the weather, pests, or plant diseases, but He could. One year all of the crops in a huge radius in our area froze in mid-August, that is, except my pumpkins. Some people call this a coinci-dence, but I call it a miracle.

As you walk through the pages of this book, you will walk with me through the years and see what it was like to walk with God. Some of the stories share a lesson learned, some share a humorous incident, and some share God's direct intervention to produce another crop and build another church. What I have done is just a drop in the bucket, but if every-one puts a drop in, pretty soon, it will be full. I hope you are inspired to have a project and become partners with God.

Prayer

"And all things, whatsoever ye shall ask in prayer, believing, ye shall receive."

— Matthew 21:22

It has been said that "Prayer is the breath of life to the soul." That is so true. I pray all the time, all day long. It is partly because I love to feel close to God and partly because I don't know what I am doing. I remember well the earnest prayer that I prayed during my first season of raising pumpkins.

I had planted one acre of pumpkins, and now, it was time to harvest them. I had a verbal agreement with the local grocery store that I would sell them 1,000 pumpkins and that I would deliver them by October 1. In North Dakota, the average frost date is September 20, so I had to pick them by that date. The only problem was that when I picked them, only 200 were fully ripe. The first thing I did was panic. The second thing I did was worry. The third thing I did was ask God to have mercy on me and somehow make these pumpkins miraculously turn orange.

I tried several different things. I placed them, one layer thick, on a long trailer and parked it in direct sunlight. One problem with this was that not nearly all of the pumpkins could fit on this trailer, and the other problem was that they would get so cold in the night that it took a long time to warm them enough during the day to make much progress.

Next, I decided to call the county agent. County agents are people who work for the government, and their job is to help farmers, or people like me in their county, who have questions on growing crops. He didn't really have an answer, so I called two more. The head extension service-man in Fargo said to me, "There is no way to ripen a green pumpkin. Throw them over the hill!"

I didn't give up. I continued to pray and to try different things. The delivery date was only one week away, and I only had 200 pumpkins ready to give them. One day, I was talking to Auntie Carol, who lived just down the road a few miles, and I mentioned my dilemma to her. Auntie Carol was a person that I really looked up to as she had a lot of experience with gardening and had the most beautiful garden around. She said with confidence, "Bring them inside, and they will ripen. Pumpkins need the temperature to be eighty degrees before they will turn color." I said, incredulously, "So do you think that if I bring them in the shop and turn the floor heat up to eighty, they will ripen?" She said, "Yes, I know they will."

Auntie Carol

I immediately got all of the pumpkins in the shop and turned on the heat. Within twenty-four hours, I could see them begin to turn color! I was thrilled! In the meantime, the produce manager of Hugo's called and said that he didn't have room for all 1,000 at once and that he would call me as he needed them.

Every time he would call, I had just enough ripe pumpkins ready to haul in, and I never told him that I had almost had to let him down. This was only the beginning of many, many miracles God performed to build churches in India. Sometimes He worked through the weather, sometimes He worked through circumstances, but this time He worked through Auntie Carol. If it hadn't been for her, there would not have been a second year of raising pumpkins. Praise God for aunties and for answered prayer!

Above All That We Ask or Think

"And try me now in this,' says the LORD *of hosts, 'If I will not open for you the windows of heaven And pour out for you such a blessing That there will not be room enough to receive it.'"*
— *Malachi 3:10, NKJV*

My first year of raising pumpkins had gone really well, so I couldn't wait to try again the next year. I had planted one acre the first year and had sold 1,100 pumpkins. Why not try two acres this year? It sounded like a good idea at the time …

The year was 2001. May 20 rolled around, and I was rearing to go! I had my hoe. I had my seeds. I had a lot of energy. With no help at all, it would take me three days to plant the whole patch, so I enlisted the help of my youngest "slave," my ten-year-old daughter. We blazed.

By the end of the second day, our muscles were so sore that we could hardly get up and down, but we pressed on. Finally, we were done, and we knelt down and prayed that God would cause the spark of life to come into these seeds and cause them to produce many, many pumpkins.

You have to be careful what you pray for! That year we harvested 5,000 pumpkins! It was a huge blessing, but how was I going to sell all of these pumpkins? As usual, the first thing I did was panic. The second thing I did was worry. And the third thing I did was pray. I was convinced that God had a plan, but it seemed a little overwhelming to think of moving that many pumpkins.

I needed customers! Lots of customers! The grocery store that bought from me the first year agreed to buy about 1,000 again this year. I still had 4,000 left. I went all over Jamestown selling pumpkins to any of the businesses that would buy from me.

Some took five, some took twenty-five, and the local bank bought 225 to share with customers as they came in. They were in the grocery stores, they were in the convenience stores, they were in the gas stations, they were at the flower shops, they were at the schools, they were everywhere! But still, I had 2,500 left.

Finally, I prayed, "Lord, I have tried as hard as I can. I don't know where else to go or who else to call. Please help me." The very next day I got a call from the manager of the Farmer's Market in Fargo. He said, "I hear you have pumpkins for sale." A thrill of anticipation surged through my body as I answered, "Yes, I do!" He said, "I'll take them all! One thousand, two thousand, whatever you've got!" As the lame man in the Bible did when Peter and John healed him, I went "walking and leaping and praising God!"

This incident, early in my career, taught me a lesson that I would need to remember during the next twenty years of partnering with God. For some reason, God seems to wait until the last possible moment, after all hope is gone, to step in to rescue His children. I learned not to look at the facts, but look at God. I learned that if He could make pumpkins, He could make customers. He has a plan, and if we will trust Him to the very end, He will do "exceedingly abundantly above all that we ask or think" (Eph. 3:20).

Thousands of Pumpkins!

Pumpkin People and Produce

"For my thoughts are not your thoughts, neither are your ways my ways, saith the LORD."

—*Isaiah 55:8*

I have good ideas, and I have bad ideas. One of my bad ideas appeared at the very beginning of my career. When I look back, I have to smile because I should have known better, but I am so thankful that God doesn't always answer our prayers with a "yes." God revealed to me a few years ago that I don't know everything, and I have listened with more of a humble heart ever since.

So what was this bad idea? I planned to sell "pumpkin people." A pumpkin person was going to basically look like a miniature snowman. I went to the second-hand store and collected outfits to dress these people in. I dressed them as Pilgrims, hippies, farmers, princesses, and many other characters. The idea was that people would want one of each of them and that they would sell like hotcakes. I got permission from the local grocery store to sell them there, and I didn't even have to give them a commission. I was going to charge ten dollars each, and I was going to make a *lot* of money for building churches in India.

It was a huge failure, and I did not sell even one "pumpkin person." The clothes I had to buy to fix them up dipped into my profit significantly, besides the fact that they were always tipping over. People weren't into pumpkin "people;" they just wanted a pretty pumpkin on their doorstep. There was only one thing that stuck after I realized that it wasn't going to work, and that was my company name—Pumpkin People and Produce. I always did think it was kind of cool that it was PPP.

What I learned from this venture was that we can trust God. When we get answers to our prayers that are unlike what we dreamed of or are working toward, instead of being sad and disappointed, we should be thankful. If God had answered my prayer the way I wanted Him to, I would have made $100 instead of $100,000.

The Bible says, "Trust in the LORD with all thine heart; and lean not unto thine own understanding. In all thy ways acknowledge him, and he shall direct thy paths" (Prov. 3:5–6).

Pumpkin People

A Cheerful Giver

"God loveth a cheerful giver."

—*2 Corinthians 9:7*

There were many decisions to make during my first year of partnering with God. How many pumpkins should I plant? How was I going to sell them? Would the grocery stores want locally grown pumpkins, or would they prefer to buy them from a warehouse? When should I plant? How was I going to control the weeds? Would they mature before frost? Like any farming venture, there were many unknowns, and finally, I had to just pull the trigger and take a chance. God had brought me this far, and I knew He wasn't going to just hang me out to dry.

The first year I decided to plant one acre of pumpkins which amounted to 400 hills containing five seeds per hill. They were planted by hand, of course, which translated into hundreds of deep-knee bends. I planted them all by myself, and it took three days, but each time I knelt to plant another hill, I was reminded that I was kneeling before the Maker of heaven and earth, and He was able to give life to these seeds and make them produce pumpkins. I sometimes dreamed of harvesting a *big* crop, and at the same time, I panicked because there might be a *big* crop.

The summer went well, and as harvest approached, I could see that there were lots and lots of pumpkins. This both thrilled me and paralyzed me with fear. How was I going to pick and wash and haul 1,000 pumpkins to town? This was *my* project, and I didn't expect help from anyone else. I had a nice surprise one day, however, when my husband couldn't harvest soybeans because it was too misty and drizzly, and he rounded up our four children to help me. My morale soared! It is really true that "Many hands make light work!"

As time went on, one of my children began to murmur and complain. It was a bit overwhelming, and this one was sick of picking pumpkins. I turned around to listen as one of their siblings piped up and said, "Don't complain, we're building a church!"

I smiled as I realized that he was right. We needed to keep our minds off the wet, soupy day and the mountain of work before us and to let our

15

imagination embrace the form of a new church in India with people eager to hear about Jesus crowded inside its walls. When we keep focused on the prize, our *ultimate* goal, we won't complain about the present circumstances. "It will be worth it all when we see Jesus."

> I saw one weary, sad, and torn,
> With eager steps press on the way,
> Who long the hallowed cross had borne,
> Still looking for the promised day;
> While many a line of grief and care,
> Upon his brow was furrowed there;
> I asked what buoyed his spirits up,
> "Oh, this!" said he, — "the blessed hope."
> — *"I Saw One Weary,"* Annie R. Smith

"Don't Complain! We're Building a Church!"

Angel Band

"For he shall give his angels charge over thee, to keep thee in all thy ways."

—*Psalm 91:11*

It was a bright, sunny day in September, and we were harvesting our seventh crop of pumpkins. Anticipation was in the air as we looked across the orange-dotted field of pumpkins. Although the weather was warm, there was a hint of fall in the air.

We were thankful for the helpers who had come to make our load lighter, and one could look out and see people cutting pumpkins, stacking pumpkins, and loading pumpkins into a large trough that a skid steer loader would bring to the wash area. There were more helpers arranged around a large, round trough filled with about three feet of water. Everyone had a scrub brush and was working and talking and laughing. Next to the wash trough was an area about six feet long where pumpkins were dried and rolled down to the end, where another worker would place them in a large cardboard bin.

The helpers were a motley crew. They ranged in age from six weeks old to ninety years old. Some adults there had never finished high school, and some were highly educated. Some were there for the social aspect, and some were there for serious work, but we valued them all! My first year, I had done it all by myself, and it took three days!

The baby that had come to "help" was asleep in her baby carrier beside the drying table when all of a sudden, a large, twenty-pound, wet, slippery pumpkin escaped the hands of a worker. People screamed, and fear gripped our hearts as we saw the pumpkin crash down on Baby Elizabeth. Miraculously, the handle of the baby carrier was up, and it absorbed the weight of the pumpkin as she continued to sleep.

We all praised the Lord for His care and protection. Just as Revelation 12:4 talks about the dragon (Satan) standing before the woman (the church), ready to devour her Child (Jesus) as soon as it was born, Satan was in my pumpkin patch that day trying to wipe out the life of an innocent baby. The beautiful thing was that she didn't even wake up. How many times are we delivered from danger or from the hands of the Enemy, and we don't even know it? I am so thankful that God sends His angels to watch over us and keep us safe.

All night, all day,
Angels watchin' over me, my Lord;
All night, all day,
Angels watchin' over me.

Angels Watched over Baby Elizabeth

Walking With God

"And Enoch walked with God."

—Genesis 5:24

I loved raising pumpkins, and I loved being partners with God. There was really not much I could do. I planted them, tilled and hoed them, and harvested and sold them, but He put the spark of life in the seeds and made them grow. He sent the sun and rain and filled the soil with nutrients. Nevertheless, I felt honored that I could have at least a small part in nurturing the plants.

Every day throughout the season, I would walk through the one-and-one-half-acre field and talk with God about "our" pumpkins. I enjoyed every stage of growth. It was a thrill to see the first leaves pop through the soil, and I pictured the pumpkins that it would produce. I was excited when the first blossom opened and when the first bees came to do their part in building a church in India. When the first walnut-sized pumpkin appeared, I rejoiced! When they got a little bigger, I would take my tape measure out to the field and measure the progress each day. A pumpkin usually grows about one inch in circumference per day, and it takes about one month to reach its full size. After that, it takes about two weeks for the skin to harden and for it to turn orange.

> *I loved raising pumpkins, and I loved being partners with God.*

Day by day, I walked and talked with God. Many times, I had goosebumps as I felt His presence near me. One summer near the beginning of my partnership with God, and when my faith was still small, I looked at the withered leaves and was concerned about the future of this crop. It was hot and dry that summer; in fact, it was the fourth driest on record. As I looked at the powdery soil and the wilting leaves, I said to God, "My pumpkins could sure use a drink of water!" Immediately, I heard Him say to me, "If I can make a pumpkin out of nothing, I can surely make a pumpkin without water!" And make pumpkins, He did! That summer, I harvested 5,000 pumpkins! It was another miracle.

That was only the beginning of my walk with God. Each year the relationship got deeper, and I thank Him for the promise of heaven when we can walk together every day, and there will be no more problems to discuss, only praise and thanksgiving.

> And He walks with me,
> And He talks with me,
> And He tells me I am His own;
> And the joy we share as we tarry there,
> None other has ever known.
> — *"In the Garden," C. Austin Miles*

Walking and Talking with God

Pepper

"But the fruit of the Spirit is ... longsuffering."

—*Galatians 5:22*

There. I thought I had everything. Purse with driver's license. Check. Statement pad. Check. Pen. Check. Four bins of pumpkins on trailer. Check. We were off!

In the early days of my partnership with God, I sold pumpkins by the pound, so I would have to stop by the grain elevator on my way to the store and weigh loaded, then stop by again on my way home and weigh empty. The difference would be the net weight, which would determine the amount I charged the store.

Daughter Mary and Pepper

It was a brisk fall day, and the wind howled through the alley at the elevator. I noticed the attendant smiling and acting especially happy. I rolled down my window, and he said, "Come, see!"

I got out of the pickup and walked to the back of the trailer, and looked into the happy brown eyes of our dog, Pepper. I exclaimed, "Pepper! What are *you* doing here?!" She wiggled with glee and wagged her tail as if to say, "I want to sell pumpkins, too!"

It was too far to take her home, so she "helped" me that day. At the store, she got lots of attention and petting.

I couldn't help but think of all the times I had been like Pepper—wagging my tail so hard it moved my whole body, so full of enthusiasm for the Lord's work. I might be at the wrong place at the wrong time, but my heavenly Father didn't scold me and punish me. He looked at my motives, my heart, and let me "ride the trailer" to town.

Thank you, God, for being patient and longsuffering with me, and please help me to always manifest the same spirit to others, even if it is a dog!

Pumpkin Sign

"Let them make Me a sanctuary; that I may dwell among them."
—Exodus 25:8

I had been raising pumpkins for many years when I received one of the most meaningful gifts of my life. My brother had just started a business in which he used a waterjet, also known as a water jet cutter. According to Wikipedia, a waterjet is "an industrial tool capable of cutting a wide variety of materials using an extremely high-pressure jet of water, or a mixture of water and an abrasive substance." Allen's machine is about eight feet by six feet and looks like a deep table filled with water. He programs into his computer a shape or design and sends the message to the machine. An extremely strong jet of water cuts through the metal or other material and makes the product.

Allen has always highly prized handmade gifts for Christmas, so he decided to make everyone in our family a present with his waterjet. That year, as we looked at all of the gifts that he had wrapped, there was one particular gift that stood out. It was about four feet tall and about three feet wide. To my surprise, the tag read, "To Cheryl." How fun! What could it possibly be? I honestly had no idea but was excited for my turn to come to open my gift.

My parents had taken seriously the command to "be fruitful and multiply," and there are thirty-six descendants, including spouses, and almost everyone shows up for Christmas. All eyes were on me as I opened the mysterious present. I tore off the paper and removed the cardboard covering. I burst into tears as I read the cut-out letters superscribed on a white church with a huge orange pumpkin background. "Let them make me a sanctuary that I may dwell among them." Exodus 25:8. I was overcome with emotion when I realized that God had allowed me to play a small part in bringing some of His faraway children close to Him in a church.

God could have let angels build a church or could have built it Himself, but He graciously chose me to be His pumpkin partner, and someday, I

23

will have the joy of seeing souls in the kingdom who worshiped in these churches. Thank You, Jesus!

Pumpkin Sign from My Brother, Allen

Geese

"My God hath sent his angel, and hath shut the lions' mouths, that they have not hurt me."

—Daniel 6:22

Every good farmer knows that you have to rotate your crops. This is necessary in order to avoid depleting the soil of certain nutrients and to avoid disease in your plants. I had three places to rotate my pumpkins, but when the water from the slough came up too high in one patch, I had to look for another.

The area where I planted my pumpkins was surrounded by water on three sides, and up a ways from the water was a U-shaped shelter belt of trees. I had always planted the pumpkins on one-half of this inside area and rotated to the other half the next year. Now that I needed a third patch, I was toying with the idea of planting pumpkins on the other side of the trees, next to the water. My husband said it would be suicide because the geese would just walk up the shore and dine on fresh green plants for breakfast, dinner, and supper. I thought about it for a long time, and since there didn't seem to be a lot of options, I decided to just pray and ask for God to protect His crop.

We had planted soybeans there before, and the geese had completely wiped them out, so I was holding my breath to see if God would do what He does best and perform another miracle. If He could shut the lions' mouths in Daniel's day, He could shut the geese's mouths in my day.

I waited and watched, and watched and waited. Day by day, my faith grew. The geese never took a bite of those beautiful pumpkin plants, and once again, there was money for another church in India. As cherubim guarded the entrance to the Garden of Eden, angels guarded the entrance to God's pumpkin patch.

Hungry Geese

Mouse!

"Keep thy heart with all diligence; for out of it are the issues of life."
—*Proverbs 4:23*

I can't think of anything good about mice. They eat the farmer's grain, they scare me, and worst of all, they would nibble on my pumpkins when they were ripe and mar their beauty. But there was one more thing they liked to do that really got me into trouble.

We had just finished harvesting another good crop of pumpkins, and I was planning to haul in the first load the next morning to Hugo's, the local grocery store that always bought my pumpkins. The shiny-clean pumpkins were all nestled in bins seated on pallets. We were ready to lift them onto the trailer with a skid steer loader the next morning, and I would be on my way. That night, however, a little mouse must have crawled up the pallet and entered the open space at the bottom of the bin. He must have thought, "Oh, heavenly bliss! Thirty pumpkins to nibble on!"

Delivering my first load of the season was always a rather festive day. People who passed me on the highway would smile as they saw my trailer of pumpkins, announcing the official beginning of fall. I pulled up to the unloading zone at the store, and as I waited to be helped, shoppers passing by would stop and admire God's handiwork, and some would even ask if they could buy some off of the trailer.

Once inside the store, they made a display of some of the bins and stored a couple of other bins in their back room. After I had left, all of a sudden, a little visitor appeared in the back room, which changed the atmosphere from peace to pandemonium. It is interesting to observe how a little creature three inches long can command everyone's undivided attention! I can only imagine the scene as they went forth to capture this little visitor.

The next time I delivered pumpkins, the produce manager told me of the excitement that had ensued after my last delivery and said that the farm mice should be kept on the farm, and they didn't want any more visitors. I apologized profusely and never took another pallet of pumpkins to a store that had been sitting out all night.

27

Sometimes we are not cautious of danger in our spiritual lives. We think some sins are little sins, just like a little mouse is a little problem, but how wrong we can be! Sin creeps into our lives as a small, silent, harmless visitor, but its results are huge. Just as I learned to guard the opening to the pumpkin bins, we must guard the door to our hearts. As the Bible says, "Keep thy heart with all diligence; for out of it are the issues of life" (Prov. 4:23).

Mouse!

Anchors

"Which hope we have as an anchor of the soul, both sure and stedfast."
—Hebrews 6:19

When I was growing up on a farm in Kansas, I knew nothing about gardening. It seems strange that gardening is now my favorite hobby! I love the feel of the soil, the smell of the soil, the looks of the soil, and pulling weeds is actually my favorite thing to do.

My mother suffered from back problems until she had surgery when I was twelve years old. Because of that, she didn't raise a garden or do much of anything strenuous. When I got married and wanted to plant a garden, my mother-in-law helped me get started and was amused but kind when she observed my lack of knowledge. For instance, I was overjoyed when I harvested my first potatoes from the garden. I had no idea that there would be more than one potato under each plant!

One thing I didn't know about pumpkins when I started raising them was that they spread out six to eight feet on each side. I questioned what would keep them from uprooting when a strong wind blew. I soon learned that each stem had something similar to roots to anchor them to the ground every few feet. It is amazing how sturdy they are when they are "tied" down.

I thought to myself, we also have an anchor that keeps us from being blown away by every wind of doctrine so that we are secure and steadfast. Christ is like the soil, full of nutrients and water and all of the things we need for perfect development. As long as we stay close to Him, we will be safe, and we will grow more and more like Him.

Ephesians 3:17–19 explains it very well when it says, "That Christ may dwell in your hearts by faith; that ye, being rooted and grounded in love, may be able to comprehend with all saints what is the breadth, and length, and depth, and height; and to know the love of Christ, which passeth knowledge, that ye might be filled with the fulness of God."

Will your anchor hold in the storms of life,
When the clouds unfold their wings of strife?
When the strong tides lift, and the cables strain,
Will your anchor drift, or firm remain?
We have an anchor that keeps the soul
Steadfast and sure while the billows roll;
Fastened to the Rock which cannot move,
Grounded firm and deep in the Savior's love.
—*Priscilla J. Owens*

Anchors are root-like structures that grow down from the stems to hold the pumpkin plant down

The Mysterious Visitor

"He said unto them, An enemy hath done this."

—*Matthew 13:28*

E very year something disastrous happened in my pumpkin patch, but every year God provided enough pumpkins to build another church. When I first started, it only took $3,500 to build a small church in India. One year I had enough to build two churches. As the cost of churches increased, my profits increased. Many years I made over $10,000.

The "designated disaster" for one year was that a mysterious visitor was eating the pumpkin seeds before they had a chance to germinate and emerge. Waiting for the pumpkins to come up had been one of my favorite things to do. I would sometimes check several times a day to see if any had made their appearance.

This year was different. Under normal conditions, you could expect to see the first over-achievers emerging by the fifth day. Others would follow, some each day, for about another week. I checked on Day 5, expecting to see some fresh, green leaves peeking through the black dirt, but there was nothing, only empty shells. I checked the next day and the next. What was the deal? I had planted 400 hills with five seeds per hill. By this time, I should be seeing hundreds of plants!

There was an interesting phenomenon that nobody could explain. Where each seed was planted, there lay the empty shell; in fact, five per hill, and in exactly the same place they were planted. There were no tracks, no clue whatsoever. We conjectured that it could have been a bird, a squirrel, or possibly a mole. We never caught anything in the very act; all we knew was that hardly any plants had come up.

As usual, the first thing I did was panic, the second thing I did was worry, and the third thing I did was pray. Eventually, God taught me to reverse the order. I decided I would try to plant more seeds, so I scrounged around the shop until I found some old seed and took a chance that it was still good. I waited another week, only to find more empty shells on top of the hills. By this time, it was June 6, and I was getting desperate. I didn't have many seeds left but planted what I had, and this time covered each hill with a plastic garbage bag until they came up.

Every year after that, I covered each hill with plastic bags, which was a lot more work, but I thanked God for giving me an idea on how to deal with this mysterious visitor. I was also thankful that God performed another miracle that year so that I would be able to sell enough pumpkins to build another church. It would be highly unlikely that pumpkins planted on the sixth of June would have time to mature, but they did!

And God also had another idea. He caused the gourds that were left in the field the year before to sprout and grow and cross-pollinate with each other so that I ended up with multiple bizarre patterns of stripes and spots and colors. They sold like crazy, and I made a lot of money from the 3,000 gourds that I accidentally produced.

"God works in mysterious ways, His wonders to perform," and He also works in mysterious ways to defeat mysterious visitors!

Empty Shells Left by the Mysterious Visitor

The Angels Must Laugh

"A time to weep, and a time to laugh."

—*Ecclesiastes 3:4*

As I mentioned earlier, the learning curve in raising pumpkins was pretty steep! I was constantly making huge mistakes, but God always had mercy and gently pointed me in the right direction, saving my life but not always my embarrassment.

One sunny day in September, I was filled with happiness as I delivered pumpkins to my special customers. Besides selling to grocery stores and the produce warehouse in Jamestown, I had personal customers who became my friends. On these trips I didn't have a full trailer load of bins, but had four or five full of different sizes of pumpkins, along with some pie pumpkins and specialty pumpkins. By the time I had stopped at three or four places, the bins were getting low. I didn't think much of it as pumpkins are heavy, right? They wouldn't go anywhere, right?

I was merrily going on my way down Highway 281, the main highway through town, and over the overpass to I-94 when I saw people looking at me in a strange way. I looked in the rearview mirror and discovered why. Several of my bins had blown over and collapsed, and there were pumpkins everywhere! Those beautiful orange balls were rolling on the highway going north, on the highway going south, and in the ditch toward the John Deere dealer. I had stopped traffic from both directions! My face turned red and my heart pounded as I pulled off onto the shoulder and scrambled out of the pickup as fast as I could. I started rescuing the pumpkins as well as clearing the road for traffic. I glanced up and saw people smiling and laughing; some of them even got out and helped me pick them up.

> *My angel must have a sense of humor to put up with me.*

I learned something that day. Actually, I learned two things. Number One: Pumpkin bins will blow over when they are not full. Number Two: My angel must have a sense of humor to put up with me. At the end of the day, if we can't look back and laugh at our mistakes as well as learn from them, we have a problem. My little mishap brought a lot of joy and probably some belly laughter to everyone witnessing the incident, and as I look back, it *was* pretty funny. I think God provides both serious and light lessons to guide us in our Christian development. As Proverbs 17:22 says, "A merry heart doeth good like a medicine."

9/11

"And he called his ten servants, and delivered them ten pounds, and said unto them, Occupy till I come."

—*Luke 19:13*

Everyone who is old enough to have a memory remembers where they were, what they were doing, and the emotions they felt when they heard the news on September 11, 2001. Wikipedia describes it like this:

> The September 11 attacks, often referred to as 9/11, were a series of four coordinated terrorist attacks by the Wahhabi terrorist group Al-Qaeda against the United States on the morning of Tuesday, September 11, 2001.

I was in Fargo trying to sell pumpkins. This was my second year of raising pumpkins, and I had more than I could handle. This was a good problem to have, but it was still a problem. My first year, I had planted one acre and sold 1,000 pumpkins. Things went so well that the second year I decided that I would try two acres. The Lord blessed me "more than I could ask or think," and I now had 5,000 pumpkins to sell. I decided to contact all of the grocery stores within a 100-mile radius and see if I could get rid of them or "reduce my inventory," as my husband would say.

The rest of my family wanted to attend the machinery show known as "Big Iron" at the edge of town, so I dropped them off, then took our vehicle and started visiting stores trying to convince them to buy my beautiful pumpkins. I had stopped at a couple of stores when I decided to pull over and call my husband for the location of one of the stores. His voice had that "bad news" tone to it; you know, the kind of sound you hear when a person is just about to tell you that someone died. He said, "I don't think you should go to any more stores. We might be in a war." Adrenaline shot through my body as I tried to process this news.

Dwight explained to me that the Twin Towers in New York City had been attacked and that a lot of people had been killed and that we didn't know what else was on the way. I abandoned my plans and drove back to the exhibit. As I walked through one of the buildings filled with booths, I felt an eerie silence as everyone was watching TV screens and the constant replay of the planes crashing into the buildings and the subsequent fires. It was terrifying. It was unbelievable. It was paralyzing. What was coming next?

In the subsequent days and months, there were some positive things that happened. People came to the Lord or rededicated their lives to Him. Church attendance soared. Patriotism flourished. "United We Stand" was seen everywhere, and there was a feeling of camaraderie. "God Bless the U.S.A." and other patriotic songs were heard on the radio as we all tried to make sense of what had happened.

As I look back, even though 9/11 wasn't the end of the world, there was a lesson in all of this for me. I asked myself, if this had been the day that Jesus was coming, what better thing could I have been doing? In the parable of the nobleman who left for a far country in Luke 19, we read that he gave each of his three servants a certain amount of money to invest or gain more money for him while he was gone, saying before he left, "Occupy (work) till I come."

As we approach the day of Jesus' second coming, let us be found working for the Lord. Let's "occupy until He comes."

The Twin Towers in New York City on September 11, 2001

Work, for the night is coming;
Work through the morning hours;
Work while the dew is sparkling;
Work 'mid springing flowers;
Work while the day grows brighter,
Under the glowing sun;
Work, for the night is coming,
When man's work is done.
— *"Work for the Night Is Coming," Anna L. Coghill*

Invasion!

*"If my people, which are called by my name, shall humble themselves,
and pray, and seek my face, and turn from their wicked ways; then will
I hear from heaven, and will forgive their sin, and will heal their land."*
—*2 Chronicles 7:14*

Every one of my pumpkin-growing years had its unique challenge, and each year, God met the challenge, and my faith grew. The Bible says that if we have faith "as a grain of mustard seed, ye shall say unto this mountain, Remove hence to yonder place; and it shall remove; and nothing shall be impossible unto you" (Matt. 17:20). One such impossible circumstance presented itself one day as I was walking and talking with God in my pumpkin patch.

It was a bright, sunny morning in early June. There was a good stand of pumpkins, and they were doing well. I was thanking God and dreaming of a bumper crop when something flew in front of me and landed on one of the pumpkin leaves. What was this strange little bug? It was small and yellow and had black stripes on its back. I stooped down for a better look and observed that there was at least one on every plant. I checked day by day and realized that the cucumber beetles had decided to hold their national convention in my field! And they were hungry! Very hungry! They were everywhere, and they were quickly destroying my beautiful plants.

As usual, the first thing I did was panic. The second thing I did was worry. And the third thing I did was pray. I began to research these evil little creatures and found that they not only eat the small plants but that they lay eggs for the next year. I quickly bought some spray and did my best to save my pumpkins. It took a long time to spray all 2,000 pumpkin plants, but I was determined to do what I could to rescue them.

I waited and watched and checked. God had answered my prayer! The cucumber beetles were dead! The plants were set back, but they were making up for lost time. They grew and grew and produced another fabulous crop.

What I learned from this incident is that even though we live in a world of sin, and even though it looks like all hope is gone, God takes care of His own, and the end result will be better than if we had not had the problem in the first place. Joel 2:25–26 says, "And I will restore to you the years that the locust hath eaten … and ye shall eat in plenty, and be satisfied, and praise the name of the LORD your God."

Have locusts eaten the years of your youth? Have locusts eaten the years of your marriage? Have locusts eaten years of your health or wealth or happiness? Take heart! He will restore to you the years you have lost.

Cucumber Beetle

Clean!

"But ye are washed, but ye are sanctified, but ye are justified in the name of the Lord Jesus, and by the Spirit of our God."
—*1 Corinthians 6:11*

Throughout the years, the most frequent comment on my pumpkins was, "They are so clean. What do you do, *wash* them?" Then their mouths would drop open upon learning that we had, indeed, washed all 3,000 or more pumpkins. Since no one else in the business did this, it set mine apart and kind of became my trademark.

I had asked the produce manager of the first store that I sold to that first year if the pumpkins needed to be washed, and he said, "No, just knock the dirt off with your glove, and that should be fine." At first, I tried that, but the washed ones looked *so* much better I just had to do it right.

It was a lot of work, but I always had help. When I first started, I still had two children at home, and they got in on a lot of washing! In those early days when we harvested pumpkins, we would load about 500 on a long trailer, pull it to the shop, unload them on the floor, and go back for another load. Each evening after school, I would round up my "slaves," and we would each wash 100 pumpkins and put them in bins. They were good sports and cheerful workers, but my daughter once told me that when she got big enough to have a mission project, it wasn't going to be pumpkins!

In the early days, we would wash each pumpkin with a bucket and rag, dry it off, and place it in a bin. My mechanical husband, who is always looking for an easier and more efficient way to do things, asked me a simple question one day that revolutionized our washing "factory." He asked, "Will a pumpkin float?" I said, "Yes." He got a twinkle in his eye and said, "I have an idea."

The next year when we harvested pumpkins, we placed the picked pumpkins in a large, round horse trough filled with water, and a group of people stood around it and scrubbed each one until it was nice and clean. Someone else took the pumpkins out of the water and laid them on a long platform where other helpers dried them and passed them down to still more helpers who placed them in bins. It worked like a charm!

When we washed pumpkins, I was always reminded of how Jesus was willing to give His life to wash away my sins. We all have a lot of mud and dirt on us from living in a world of sin and from making bad choices, but He gently holds each one of us and washes us clean.

Are you washed in the blood?
In the soul-cleansing blood of the Lamb?
Are your garments spotless, are they white as snow?
Are you washed in the blood of the Lamb?
—*E. A. Hoffman*

Shiny, Clean Pumpkins!

Friendly Fire

"Therefore be patient, brethren, until the coming of the Lord. See how the farmer waits for the precious fruit of the earth ... you also be patient."

—James 5:7–8, NKJV

As the song says, "Nobody knows the trouble I've seen," nobody really does. I have had multiple catastrophes related to weather, weeds, viruses, pests, and other factors, but I think the hardest for me to take was "friendly fire," the problems that I brought on myself. It was kind of like an autoimmune disease, where the body makes its own self sick.

One particular year had gotten off to a good start, and the plants were growing nicely. They were very healthy, and the large, green leaves looked like hundreds of elephant ears swaying in the warm, gentle breeze. The only problem was that the weeds were just as healthy.

My husband, always trying to make my pumpkin farming less labor-intense, suggested that instead of hoeing around two thousand plants, we should just spray around them with a weed-killer. I was a little apprehensive, wondering if it would accidentally get on the leaves and kill the plants; however, I trusted him. After all, he was a successful farmer and used chemicals all of the time. He was actually going to do the spraying, and all I would have to do is drive along beside him on the four-wheeler, carrying the little sprayer.

My fears were realized when the plants turned a light green and just quit growing. They did not live and they did not die. I quit checking on them. It was too painful. I beat myself up for agreeing to try such a risky operation. I wished a hundred times I could be out there hoeing and doing something I knew how to do. I didn't say much as my husband felt just as bad as I did. There was nothing I could do but wait.

About the first of August, I got up my courage and walked through my field. I wasn't sure, but I thought there was a spark of life. A few days later, I confirmed my wildest dream! They had started growing again! They later bloomed and produced pumpkins. We were going to have another church after all!

Besides learning that God has mercy on us when we accidentally make wrong decisions, I also learned to never give up, to never stop praying. Sometimes we don't understand God's delays, but He can see the future just as clearly as he can see the past, and He has a plan all worked out. There is a reason that the Bible says, "Wait on the LORD" (Ps. 37:34).

The Plants Would Not Live, and They Would Not Die

I'm Going to Sell Them!

"I can do all things through Christ which strengtheneth me."
—*Philippians 4:13*

During the twenty-one years that I sold pumpkins to the local grocery store called Hugo's, I dealt with five different produce managers. Connie was Produce Manager Number Four. All of the managers were great to work with, but what I loved about Connie was her love to sell. A woman after my own heart!

Connie had a happy face and a quick wit. She was personable and friendly, and I liked her immediately. She was always busy and did her job well. I sold her mini pumpkins, gourds, large decorative pumpkins, and pie pumpkins. She had a beautiful display that never reflected the dark side of Halloween but the beautiful side of fall.

Pie pumpkins are about the size of a cantaloupe and are sweeter and less stringy than the large, decorative pumpkins and are better for making pies; thus, their name. In a normal year, I would sell about 2,000 pie pumpkins, besides the other produce. This year, however, God outdid Himself, and I had 5,000 to sell! They were almost all ripe, and they were gorgeous, but I was scared. I said to God, "I know You have great confidence in me, but 5,000—really?" We had picked all day and washed by the light of the silvery moon. Finally, all of my helpers mutinied on me, and still, there were pumpkins left in the field. A few people came back the next day, and we finished picking, and God also sent a couple of faithful neighbors over who helped us finish washing them, but now came the hard part—selling them!

While we were still picking, my oldest son suggested we quit and leave some of them in the field. He said, "Why should we pick all of these? You can never sell them all!" That was just the challenge I needed! I knew it was twice as many as I had ever sold before, but I also had many years of experience in witnessing God's miracles under my belt. I calmly replied, "I will sell them."

I called every grocery store within a 100-mile radius, and I sold and sold and sold, but I still had a lot of pumpkins left. I decided to contact Cammy, the produce manager for all eleven stores of the Hugo's chain located in Grand Forks, to see if any of the other stores could use pie pumpkins. The large, decorative pumpkins are much more popular and are easy to sell, but pie pumpkins are small and much harder to sell. Cammy caught the spirit and loved my building-a-church-in-India project anyway, so she *strongly* urged all of the stores to purchase at least one bin (about 150 pumpkins). Even though the Jamestown store was one of the smaller stores in the chain, Connie sold by far the most pumpkins. When she ordered six bins (900 pumpkins), I was thrilled but asked her what she was going to do with that many pumpkins. She said in her spunky way, "I'm going to sell them!" And she did! God blessed her, and God blessed me.

Once again, my faith grew, and I couldn't wait to tell my son that I had, indeed, sold them all!

Connie's Pie Pumpkins for Sale

Sin Stinks

"For mine iniquities are gone over mine head: as an heavy burden they are too heavy for me. My wounds stink and are corrupt because of my foolishness."

—Psalm 38:4–5

I am a "smell" person. I love smells! Smells make me happy! I have scented candles burning all winter, and I have never met a scent I didn't like. I enjoy the smell of fresh bread baking, sugar cookies in the oven, and the nostalgic smell of a freshly-cut cedar tree at Christmastime. I like perfume, bubble bath, the smell of flowers, the smell of rain, the smell of the good earth. I believe that God did not have to create us with the sense of smell but did so as kind of a bonus. It adds pleasure to our lives.

But just as following God is like a good smell, *sin stinks.* Satan has perverted all the good things that God has made. God made only happiness and good smells. Satan caused things to creep into the good things of life, the good smells, and his odors stink so much that they often completely drown out God's original smells.

Each year when pumpkin harvest is complete, and all of the pumpkin bins are neatly lined up in the shop, it smells good. It smells like pumpkins. It smells like success. It smells like there will be a new church in India. However, just as the perfect happiness of heaven was soon broken by the entrance of sin, so the perfect smell of pumpkins is soon tainted by the stench of rotting pumpkins, the smell of sin.

> *When we smell sin in our lives, we need to remove it so it won't control our whole lives and stink up our environment.*

With 3,000-5,000 pumpkins in the shop, there are bound to be a few rotten ones, and their smell overpowers the smell of the good ones. Sin stinks. No matter how good a pumpkin might look and smell in the beginning, if it has a broken stem, a bruise, or insect damage, it will rot, and it will stink.

47

When we smell sin in our lives, we need to remove it so it won't control our whole lives and stink up our environment. God has promised to forgive our sins and remove iniquity from us so that we will be a sweet-smelling savor to Him and to everyone around us. Just as the fragrance of the ointment that Mary poured on Jesus' feet filled the whole room, even so, when a Christian comes into the room, it should be evident that Jesus' love is radiating from people's faces.

Sin stinks. Jesus can remove sin and its stench from our lives so that we will be one with Him.

"And walk in love, as Christ also hath loved us, and hath given himself for us an offering and a sacrifice to God for a sweetsmelling savor" (Eph. 5:2).

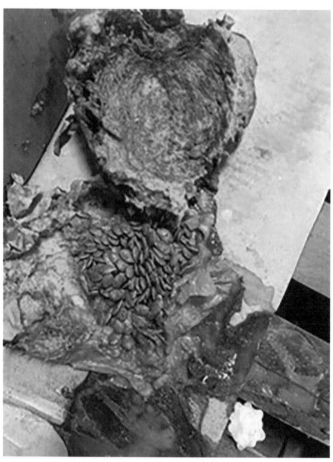

Sin Is Like a Rotting Pumpkin

Gourds

"He has made everything beautiful …"

—*Ecclesiastes 3:11, NKJV*

Besides raising pumpkins, I also raised gourds. Every gourd is different, and every gourd is beautiful. In fact, I never met a gourd I didn't like. Some are large, some are small, and some are in-between. Some are green, some are orange, some are yellow, and they also come in every sort of combination of colors, stripes, and spots. Some look like swans, some look like eggs, and some look like miniature pumpkins. Some are bumpy, and some are smooth. When my mother-in-law and I would stand by the sink, washing thousands of gourds, we never ceased to be amazed at the variety and the beauty.

Gourds were not a money-making venture for me; I sold them three-for-a-dollar, but I always raised some anyway, just because it wouldn't be

Uniquely Beautiful Gourds

fall without gourds. I felt that their bright colors and cheerful faces could make anyone smile.

As I looked at the thirty boxes of shiny-clean, colorful creations of God, I was drawn to a lesson that God was trying to teach me. In Genesis 1:31, we read that at the end of Creation, "God saw every thing that He had made, and, behold, it was very good." This includes every type of person and personality. We are all part of a huge puzzle, and every piece is important. Every person contributes something to the world that makes it special. Life would be very dull if we all looked alike, if we were all orange-striped gourds if you will, but God in His wisdom has made us all different. We need to appreciate each other's unique qualities, and we need to strive to see the beauty in every person in the same way that *God* does when He looks at us. "And everybody's beautiful in their own way. Under God's Heaven, the world's gonna find the way." —Ray Stevens

Unspotted

"Can there any good thing come out of Nazareth?"

—*John 1:46*

When Jesus began to become popular, many people were probably asking the question that Nathanael had asked, "Can there any good thing come out of Nazareth?" While it is true that "one bad apple can spoil the barrel," it doesn't have to be that way. I saw this lesson vividly portrayed in my pumpkin business.

Looking out on the orange-dotted, one-and-one-half acre field of pumpkins on harvest day was thrilling. Anticipation was in the air, and I was anxious to finally get the crop to safety inside my shop where there would no longer be the threat of damage or ruin to God's pumpkins.

We only picked the near-perfect pumpkins, and if there was even a hint that one might spoil, we left it in the field. When their clean, shiny faces looked at me from their neat pumpkin bins, you would never guess that about 3 percent of them would spoil. That is just life on Planet Earth.

The thing that I learned from rotting pumpkins, however, made a huge impression on my spiritual life. This is just it: You don't have to be negatively influenced by your environment. You don't have to decay and spoil just because everything or everyone around you is decaying and spoiling. You don't have to give in to peer pressure.

After harvest day, all of the pumpkins would be carefully waiting in their forty-pumpkin bins to be delivered to the warehouse or to the local grocery stores. But before I would deliver them, I would always take them out, one by one, and make sure that there was no sign of spoilage or hint that it might happen later. I did my best to deliver perfect pumpkins, representative of my God's ability to produce spectacular fruit.

There are many things that can cause a pumpkin to rot. Sometimes the person loading the pumpkin in the field might drop it instead of gently laying it in the tank, and it would begin to rot from the inside. Other times, the stem might get broken off, and the pumpkin would start to rot in that area. Also, insects can make little bites in the skins when they are tender, and spoilage can be set in motion then.

Sometimes the top of a bin would look perfect, but I would see flies congregating there, or see a pool of liquid on the floor, indicating that one pumpkin in the bin had started to decompose. This always struck fear in my heart, and I was happy to dispose of the offender. I always said that if pumpkins were going to spoil, they needed to do it in my shop and not in the store!

I would take off the pretty pumpkins on top and search for a decomposed, rotting pumpkin that had the smell and consistency of diarrhea. The interesting thing was that even though the rotten pumpkin was touching several other pumpkins and may have actually dripped its disgusting goo on its friends, the healthy pumpkins were not affected. I simply had to wash them in a little soap and water, and they never told anyone that they had been associating with bad company.

What I learned is that just as healthy pumpkins are sometimes put in a bin with one that will rot and decompose, we also might be put in the company of ungodly people. The lesson is that we don't have to succumb. We don't have to fold to peer pressure. We don't have to break down and die. If we saturate ourselves in God's Word and live a life of prayer, we will still shine no matter what happens. "Pure religion undefiled before God and the Father is this … to keep himself unspotted from the world" (James 1:27).

Unspotted by Sin

A Thrilling Ride!

"For the LORD thy God is with thee whithersoever thou goest."
—*Joshua 1:9*

In North Dakota, winter can come early, and almost every October, I had to make at least one pumpkin delivery in the snow. I am not much of a manly-man, and pulling a trailer full of pumpkins was always a little scary for me, especially in inclement weather. Before I left, I always prayed that God would keep me safe and help me drive well.

Snow had fallen the day before, and the gravel roads were slushy and slick. I was nervous about driving to town and took it easy going up and down the many hills on the way. I was thankful that the trailer kept following along nicely, and I breathed a sigh of relief as I pulled into the unloading zone at the grocery store. I let the produce manager know that I had arrived, and she, in turn, notified the designated unloaders. They were not *particularly* happy to see me as they didn't like to unload in the snow any more than I did, but soon they came out the door of the store with the floor jack that they affectionately called the "dinosaur." It was old and clubby but could get the job done if someone had remembered to plug in the battery the night before.

Once unloaded, I hopped in the pickup and said another quick prayer for protection. The roads were more packed down now and even slicker than when I had gone in. It was difficult to get up the hills, and as I was coming down one such hill, my trailer started fish-tailing, which caused me to lose control, and the pickup and trailer headed for the ditch. Surprisingly, I didn't scream but just kept driving through the edge of my neighbor's sunflower field until I popped out and drove back up the ditch. As my husband would say, "You don't have to go to the fair to have a thrilling ride!"

When I realized I was back on the road, that I wasn't stuck, and that I hadn't hurt the pickup or trailer, I just kept driving and prayed that I wouldn't have another experience like that until I got home. Other than high blood pressure and a few heart palpitations, I was fine, but now came the embarrassing part. I was going to have to go to the neighbor and 'fess up to driving through the edge of his field and offer to pay for damages. Russell, a great supporter of my pumpkin project, just laughed and brushed away my offer to make things right, saying that a bag of my garden cucumbers (his favorite food) would be sufficient payment!

God has a plan for each day, and as we get up in the morning and dedicate our lives to Him, He will make sure that His plan is realized, even though it may not happen in the way *we* had planned. He promised that He would go with me wherever I went, and I felt like He was with me that day. I'm sure the angels smiled as they were called on to push me up out of the ditch that day, and I am thankful for the safe, thrilling ride in my own personal "amusement park!"

A Thrilling Ride Through My Neighbor's Sunflower Field

Boomers

"Be sober, be vigilant; because your adversary the devil, as a roaring lion, walketh about, seeking whom he may devour."
—1 Peter 5:8

Most people think deer are beautiful. They are—in the right setting, but just as a plant out of place is called a weed, an animal out of place is called a pest.

After our dog Pepper died, the deer felt like it was their turn to rule our farm. They even got so tame that they would look in our kitchen window!

The crop year of 2020 was looking good, and we were past the threat of clearwing moths, cucumber beetles, anthracnose, and other problems that commonly endanger pumpkins. I thought we were home free until I

A Boomer Fires Every Few Minutes to Scare Away Animals

discovered that our deer "friends" had started helping themselves to the green pumpkins, appetizers, if you will, before the ripe, orange ones.

About the only way to control deer is to get a dog, but since the mama dog we were hoping to get a puppy from had only one puppy, and it died, we were out of luck.

One day, my husband suggested we set up a boomer on the edge of my field. A boomer is basically a small propane tank that is set to ignite a tiny bit of gas every few minutes and make a loud bang similar to the shooting of a gun. We didn't think of explaining to our nearest neighbors who lived a few miles away that we had set this up, and they were wondering if there had been a hold-up at our place!

As it turned out, there *was* a hold-up! Satan was being held up for trying to destroy my means of building another church in India. He was forced to retreat and take the pumpkin-eating deer with him! There is more than one way to "put on the whole armor of God" (Eph. 6:11)!

Weeds

"Thorns also and thistles shall it bring forth to thee."

—Genesis 3:18

Pumpkins are large, strong plants and are very competitive, being able to shade out most common weeds if given a head start. There is one weed, however, that poses a big problem for pumpkins—the Canada thistle. After fighting them for many years, I became painfully aware of the sad consequences of the sin of our first parents in the Garden of Eden. "Cursed is the ground for thy sake," God said to Adam, and the human race has suffered ever since.

I knew that this weed was particularly hard, if not impossible, to control, and after reading about it, I learned why. Not only does it produce seeds, 1,000-1,500 seeds per *one* flowering stem, and there are many stems per plant, it also spreads through its roots. Horizontal roots may extend

Canada Thistle—The Impossible Weed

fifteen feet or more, and vertical roots may grow six to fifteen feet deep. It sounded like "checkmate" to me!

While the pumpkins were small, I could till between the rows with my little tractor and pull-behind tiller. When I would finish, the soil would be black and perfect and there would not be a weed in sight. Most weeds were polite enough to not re-emerge and would even show their withered leaves and roots on the ground. However, thistles were different. It wasn't long before I would see little green shoots coming up even thicker than before. This weed was clearly associated with Satan! With roots fifteen feet below the soil, there was little chance of truly conquering this weed. As my husband would say, "Weeds can be controlled with a great amount of effort for a short amount of time."

Because of sin and its effects, "the whole creation groaneth and travaileth in pain" (Rom. 8:22). Each day as I dealt with these thistles, I was reminded that "In this world ye shall have tribulation: but be of good cheer; I have overcome the world" (John 16:33). I learned that tribulation and dealing with thistles is a part of life on Planet Earth, but it will not always be that way. Better days are coming. Isaiah 65:17 says, "Behold, I create new heavens and a new earth: and the former shall not be remembered, nor come into mind."

Lord, Help Me!

"Even a fool who keeps silent is considered wise."
—*Proverbs 17:28, ESV*

Many times in my pumpkin career, I found myself doing things that were a little above my skill level, and I had to do a lot of praying. I didn't feel comfortable pulling a trailer load of pumpkins to Jamestown, much less Fargo. Besides that, I am not good at finding my way around, and my husband even says that I was born without a compass! I am not naturally mechanical, and one time when I was helping with the trucking on the farm at harvesttime, I couldn't make it up a steep hill with a truck loaded with grain. When I put the clutch in to shift to a lower gear, it just started rolling faster and faster backward down the hill, and I found myself saying the words, "God, have mercy on me," repeatedly as I swerved between the two ditches. When I got to the bottom of the hill and discovered that I had not killed myself or wrecked the truck, I put it in first gear and took all the time I needed to go up that hill.

Experiences like this made me lean all the heavier on the Lord for help when hauling pumpkins to my stores. When I first started, I sold pumpkins by the pound, so I would have to stop by the elevator on the way in to Fargo and ask them to weigh me full, and then stop back and ask them to weigh me empty so I would have a net weight to charge the store. I very quickly discovered that if I were just myself and admitted that I didn't know what I was doing, people would be really nice to me. Like when I pulled up to the elevator for the first time and went in and asked if they would be so kind as to weigh my pumpkins, they took a look out the window and smiled at such a bizarre break in their day and gladly showed me where to drive and what to do.

> *I very quickly discovered that if I were just myself and admitted that I didn't know what I was doing, people would be really nice to me.*

When I first delivered pumpkins to the Hornbacher stores in Fargo, they told me where to back my trailer up to the unloading dock. I smiled and said, "I don't back trailers," and handed them the keys. They were so nice and did a great job. I think they sensed that if they had let me do it, they would have been there for a few hours!

I got lost one day, too. Here I was, before the days of GPS, pulling a trailer and driving all around a residential district in Fargo with a load of pumpkins. I panicked when I realized I had entered a cul-de-sac. Knowing my backing skills, I was sure that backing up wasn't an option. Going forward didn't look too promising either. I prayed, and God helped me get that rig turned around. I'm not saying that I might not have run over a right curb or two, but I didn't have an accident or cause an accident to happen.

What I learned from all of this was that if God calls you to do something, He is going to actually help you do it. He might help you in the form of putting people in your path to have mercy on you or choose some other way, but He *will* help you. I also learned that when you are honest and humble, people are more than happy to lend a hand. As the song says, "It's me, it's me, it's me, oh Lord, standin' in the need of prayer! It's me, it's me, it's me, oh Lord, standin' in the need of prayer."

Prayer Changes Things

A Well-Oiled Machine

*"For as the body is one, and hath many members of that one body, ...
so also is Christ.*

—*1 Corinthians 12:12*

As the years rolled by, our pumpkin-picking operation became more and more sophisticated and efficient, thanks to my husband, who had a talent for logistics and order. I *love* to work as a team, and pumpkin harvest day was the highlight of my year. We would pick, rain or shine, and people learned to prepare for a long but fun day.

It reminded me of a hive of bees. There are many bees, and each one knows its job and is happy to do it. Without the queen bee to lay eggs, the colony would soon die out. Without the worker bees to search for food, keep the hive clean, care for the young, and guard the hive, the colony would soon die out. Without the drones, or male bees, to mate with the queen bee, the colony would soon die out.

In the pumpkin patch, it takes many people working hard to make the day a success. Every job is important, and without everyone working together toward one goal, the day would be a failure.

If a helicopter would fly over the pumpkin patch on harvest day, this is what the pilot would see. All over the field, he would observe workers cutting the pumpkins with hack saws or large loppers. Then another team would be seen gathering the pumpkins into piles of about twenty-five pumpkins. Next, a skid steer loader with an oblong watering trough would be observed coming to the piles of pumpkins, and workers would be loading them into the trough to be taken back to another large, round trough filled with water. About ten helpers would be seen standing around the round trough, using a scrub brush to clean the pumpkins. One strong person would be lifting the pumpkins out of the water and placing them on a long table-like structure padded with towels, and about six people would be drying them. The pumpkins would then be rolled down the table to the "foreman," who would be in charge of sorting the pumpkins into bins of ripe or green ones.

When the bins were full, another skid steer loader would come and load them onto a long trailer that would hold up to fourteen bins. The trailer would be hooked up to a pickup that would take the pumpkins back to the shop, where another small tractor would unload the trailer and place them in an orderly fashion inside the shop.

There was also one more job which is often overlooked, but was probably the most important job of all—cooking! The ladies who had small children or were not physically able to work in the field volunteered to feed the sixty hungry workers who came in for dinner and supper. After prayer, we would *cheer* for these ladies!

As I took part in this operation, I was reminded of a well-oiled machine running smoothly, with each part contributing to the success of the mission. All of a sudden, it occurred to me that God has called His church to be a well-oiled machine, ready and willing to do whatever He asks us to do to promote His kingdom. In the pumpkin patch, not everyone could drive equipment, but they could all work. There was work for the four-year-olds, just as there was work for the ninety-year-olds! There was work for both men and women, children and youth, strong and weak.

The Body of Christ Has Many Members

God is calling you to be part of the body of Christ. You might not be the brain or the eye or a strong muscle, but even toes are important in God's work! God's church, Christ's body, will not be the same without you. When He says, "Whom shall I send, and who will go for us?" will you answer, "Here am I; send me" (Isa. 6:8)?

Cammy

"Greater love hath no man than this, that a man lay down his life for his friends."

—John 15:13

ammy. I loved the name and soon learned to love the person. Who was this spunky new lady in the produce department? She had dark hair and pretty brown eyes that had a special sparkle. Soon I was introduced to her and learned that she was the new produce director over all eleven Hugo's stores. Her job was to visit all the stores and help the produce managers do the best job possible. I could tell she was good at her job. She worked with energy and efficiency, yet made you feel that she had all the time in the world to talk to you. As time went on, I could tell that she was a strong Christian, and I learned a lot from her.

I could tell we were kindred spirits, and our friendship grew on a personal as well as a business level during the next few years. It was always a treat to see her on the days that she worked with the Jamestown store. When she learned that my pumpkins were "missionary" pumpkins, she did all she could to help me sell them and promote the project. When she learned that I wanted to put my pumpkin experiences into a collection of stories for a book, she said, "I think you will inspire everyone to be better. In times like these, we all need some good stories to help us get through. You, my friend, are a good story. Stay healthy and keep spreading love and happiness." That's the way she was, always thinking of others and always very encouraging.

She drove a hard bargain and wanted to buy pumpkins for as little as possible, yet she sold thousands of them for me by her influence. When I had 5,000 pie pumpkins to sell, twice as many as I usually had, and I had exhausted every avenue that I could think of, I turned to her for help. She said, "Give me a few minutes to contact all of the stores, and I will get back with you." She sold them all!

Toward the end of my last season, I had twenty bins left to sell, and I called Cammy to see if she would like some for the other stores. Unlike Cammy, she didn't get back to me until later that day. She said, "I am sorry I missed this. I had surgery today to donate a kidney. Very sleepy yet. Will call soon." She did call soon and bought them all! I couldn't believe that just hours before she had donated a kidney to the sister of her sister-in-law, and she was thinking of helping me out! She explained that when she heard that this lady was going to die without a kidney transplant, she immediately offered to be tested to see if she was a match. It turned out that she was a *perfect* match! I couldn't believe that she had gone through all of that for someone who wasn't even a blood relative. That was Cammy. The last time I communicated with her she was sitting by the side of her dying mother, once again making someone else's life better.

I believe that God put Cammy in my life to teach me what serving others and advancing God's kingdom through ordinary life events looked like. She must have read what Jesus said in Matthew 25:40, "Inasmuch as ye have done it unto one of the least of these my brethren, ye have done it unto me." Thank you, Cammy!

Cammy and Cheryl

Miracle Muscles

"I can do all things through Christ which strengtheneth me."
—Philippians 4:13

During my twenty-one years of raising pumpkins, I experienced dozens of miracles. I think it is a miracle when clearwing moths destroy two-thirds of your plants, and you still have enough pumpkins to build a church. I think it is a miracle when all of the baby seedlings freeze off, and they come back and still produce enough pumpkins to build a church. I think it is a miracle when all of the pumpkins in

"I have lifted over one million pounds of pumpkins and have never hurt my back."

the area freeze at harvesttime, and the church pumpkins are spared. I think it is a miracle when severe drought is in the land, and the pumpkins are unaffected. I think it is a miracle when cucumber beetles destroy hundreds of small plants, and you still have enough pumpkins for a church. I could go on and on.

There is one miracle, however, that I didn't give much thought to until I sat down and did the math. God has gifted me with lots of energy. I mean *lots* of energy, and when it comes to doing projects for the Lord, I have almost super-human energy. I have always said that God gives everyone brains or energy, and I got energy! But in addition to energy, He has given me a strong body.

I am very scrawny, and you would never guess that God has blessed me with strength. Conservatively speaking, I have lifted over one million pounds of pumpkins and have never hurt my back or any other muscle for that matter. What a miracle! I believe God gave me special strength, miracle muscles if you will, to carry out the purpose He had for providing churches for all of those new Christians in India. Just as God strengthened David to fight Goliath, and just as God strengthened Samson so he could fight the enemies of Israel, I believe He strengthened me.

Church Parade

"I was glad when they said unto me, Let us go into the house of the LORD.*"*

—*Psalm 122:1*

My beautiful maroon sari stuck to my sweaty body as I made my way to the highly decorated ox cart prepared for the group of Maranatha volunteers who were on their way to the dedication ceremony of the "pumpkin" church. Excitement was in the air as we anticipated the parade, and happiness filled my heart as I pictured a group of new believers sitting on the floor of their new church, worshiping God with hearts of love and gratitude for what He had done for them.

Church Parade

I was told that the people of the villages would not respect a religion in which there was no building for worship, thus the motivation for me to build as many churches as possible. The new church would also be the nicest building in town.

Finally, after traveling over many bumpy roads, we reached the church. A crowd of people had gathered to meet the parade. A conference official and a local pastor sat up front in the only chairs available in the new house of worship. We heard what the Americans had said, and then a translator told us what the Indian people had said. At last, came the moment of unveiling the plaque of dedication on the front of the church. As I cut the ribbon, a thrill swept through me while everybody cheered. Was it just humans that I heard, or were there angels in the crowd as well?

What Is That in Your Hand?

"And the LORD said unto him, What is that in thine hand?"
—Exodus 4:2

I f you are like me, you don't feel like you are anything special, and that after you're gone, there won't be a building, football stadium, or even a city street named after you. I remember that one of the U.S. presidents talked a lot about what his legacy would be. He wanted to be noticed and remembered for something that would last forever.

After Moses left the limelight and became a nobody-shepherd, he was reticent to answer God's call to lead the children of Israel out of Egypt. When God said in Exodus 3:10, "Come now therefore, and I will send thee unto Pharaoh, that thou mayest bring forth my people the children of Israel out of Egypt," Moses answered in verse 11 by saying, "Who am I that I should go unto Pharaoh?" God answered, "Certainly I will be with thee" (verse 12).

Moses continued arguing with the Lord and said in Exodus 4:10, "O my LORD, I am not eloquent, neither heretofore, nor since thou hast spoken unto thy servant: but I am slow of speech, and of a slow tongue." God was so patient with Moses and said, "Who hath made man's mouth? ... Now therefore, go, and I will be with thy mouth, and teach thee what thou shalt say" (verses 11-12).

Earlier, in Exodus 4:1–2, when Moses said, "But behold, they will not believe me, nor hearken unto my voice,"

> ***God asks each one of us, "What is that in your hand?"***

God asked, "What is that in your hand?" He answered that it was a rod, but when God told him to throw it down, it turned into a snake. Just so with us. God asks each one of us, "What is that in your hand?" We are put on this earth to praise God and to help people. What can you do to bless others?

God has a work for everyone to do, and I think He wants us to do something that we enjoy. Stop reading and think a minute. What do you really like to do? How can that be channeled in a direction to help others? I love to garden and work with plants, so raising pumpkins was an easy fit. I also love manual labor and getting dirty and sweaty, so that also is a fit. I am an extrovert and love being with people, and I especially love selling. Bingo! Another fit!

But what do you like to do? Do you like to work with wood? Maybe you could build birdhouses and sell them for a project. Do you like to bake? Maybe you could make muffins or bread and sell them for missions. Do you like to crochet? Maybe you could make baby blankets and give them to single mothers. The possibilities are endless! The main thing is that you *use* the thing that is in your hand, because as He has said, "Certainly I will be with thee" (Exod. 3:12).

Let God Use Whatever Is in Your Hands

The End, or a New Beginning?

"For I know the thoughts that I think toward you, says the LORD, thoughts of peace and not of evil, to give you a future and a hope."
—Jeremiah 29:11, NKJV

This afternoon, October 22, 2020, Pumpkin People and Produce officially closed. I cleaned up my pumpkin patch for the last time and hauled off my last bin of green pumpkins that were too immature to sell. As I walked up the hill to the patch, a flood of memories filled my soul. I paused a moment to reflect, reminisce, and recall the sounds, smells, and emotions of the past twenty-one pumpkin harvests.

I pictured a crowd of sixty to seventy people working together like a well-oiled machine, but at the same time talking, laughing, and dreaming of another church building in India. In my mind's eye, I saw people cutting pumpkins, people loading pumpkins into the large horse trough, a skid steer loader bringing them to the water to be washed, people scrubbing and pleasantly talking, people drying, people loading them into bins, and finally, the pickup truck pulling a trailer load of orange pumpkins to the shop to be stored until delivery. I had a lump in my throat and a few tears as I thought of India and the people I had met there and their parade through the streets, showing their excitement as they walked to their new church.

Then I was overwhelmed with the realization that God had allowed me, unworthy though I was, to partner with Him in this tiny part of His work. I thought of the thrill of seeing the plants come up, witnessing the first blossom of the season, and then the bright, cheerful pumpkins which would brighten people's doorsteps and signal the beginning of fall. It was amazing to think that a handful of seeds could turn into a church.

I knelt down right in the field, as I had done so many times during this twenty-one-year journey, and thanked God for the privilege of working with Him and for the lessons in faith I had learned. We had been through

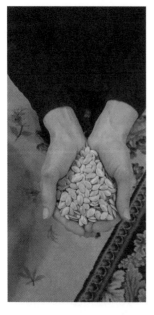

a lot together—soil so wet it couldn't be cultivated, soil so dry I wondered how I could get a crop, cucumber beetles, animals eating the seeds before they came up, a worm that could burrow into the vine and kill a perfectly healthy plant, early frosts, hail, and more—and He was always faithful. I always had enough pumpkins to sell to our local grocery store, and usually many, many more. "Our God is an awesome God."

As I talked with Him and looked up into the dark clouds that filled the sky, I saw a patch of blue and pictured God looking down on me kneeling in His field, and I asked, "What now, Lord? Do you have another assignment for me? 'Here am I; send me.'" Isaiah 6:8

Seeds to Churches—God's Miracle in the Pumpkin Patch!

During my twenty-one years in the pumpkin patch with God, I was able to earn almost $200,000 and help build twenty-five churches.

Dwight and Cheryl Erickson

TEACH Services, Inc.
P U B L I S H I N G

We invite you to view the complete
selection of titles we publish at:
www.TEACHServices.com

We encourage you to write us
with your thoughts about this,
or any other book we publish at:
info@TEACHServices.com

TEACH Services' titles may be purchased in
bulk quantities for educational, fund-raising,
business, or promotional use.
bulksales@TEACHServices.com

Finally, if you are interested in seeing
your own book in print, please contact us at:
publishing@TEACHServices.com
We are happy to review your manuscript at no charge.